GW00537024

英語訳付き

寿司

ガイドブック

THE SUSHI
MENU BOOK

Ikeda Publishing　③池田書店

はじめに

　ニューヨーク、パリ、ミラノなど、今、世界中で人気を高める日本の食文化の神髄・寿司。

　本書は、白身、赤身、光り物、その他の魚介、ちらし、巻物、つまみ、汁物などを含む全52種を、日本語と英語で解説。魚介の生態から名前の由来、旨味の秘密、食べ方などを網羅、さらに寿司の歴史、マナー、材料、寿司に合う酒を加え、まさに寿司に関するあらゆる情報がひと目でわかる。

　寿司には、注文の仕方、味わい方に、食べる人の品格が表れる。外国の人々にも寿司を通じ、日本の文化を学べる一冊である。

Preface

Sushi, the essence of Japanese food culture, is now increasingly popular in New York, Paris, Milan, and all over the world.

This book examines fifty-two topics in English and Japanese, including white meat, red meat, silver-skinned fish, other seafood, chirashi-zushi, maki-mono (rolls), tsumami (appetizer), and shiru-mono (soups). You can find at a glance everything you need to know about sushi, ranging from the ecology of fish, to the origin of its name, the secret of its delicious taste, how to eat it, and even its history, sushi etiquette, ingredients, and which sake complements sushi.

The way a person orders sushi and enjoys its flavor reveals that person's character. This book aims to help people outside Japan learn about Japanese culture through sushi.

Contents

目次

本書の見方
How to Use at this Book

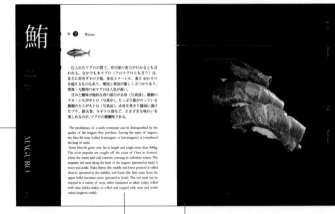

魚の名前（ローマ字）
寿司店での注文に役立ちます。

●Name of fish
(Roman alphabet)
This is useful when ordering
at a sushi restaurant.

●寿司の写真
左側で解説した寿司の写真です。寿司店で、この写真を指差せば、簡単に注文することもできます。

●Picture of sushi
An explanation of the sushi is given at the left.
You can easily order this sushi at a restaurant
if you show the picture.

●解説
それぞれの寿司ダネの味わいや歯ごたえ、旬や産地、食する部位や調理法による味の違いなどを詳しく解説。読むだけで、寿司の美味しさが広がります。

●Explanation
This provides a detailed explanation of the various kinds of
sushi, including information about toppings, texture, when
seafood is in season, where it is harvested, what parts are eaten,
and how flavors differ according to how it is prepared. Just
reading this explanation will increase your enjoyment of sushi.

第一章

寿司を美味しく食べる

Chapter 1
How to Enjoy
Eating Sushi

THE SUSHI
MENU BOOK

テンプラ、スキヤキと並び、寿司は世界中でますます人気を高めている日本食。米、魚、野菜といった新鮮な食材を使った低カロリー・低脂肪のヘルシーさがその人気の理由である。

寿司とは一般的には、ご飯に酢と塩を混ぜ、魚介をのせて握る「江戸前握り寿司」のことだが、その歴史は江戸時代の終わり頃（1800年初頭）まで遡る。屋台で注文して立ったまま食べる、手軽で便利なファストフードとして当時の人々に愛された。

修業を積んだ職人の技が光るのが寿司。旬の魚を目利きし、最適な方法で素材を扱い、漬ける・炙る・煮るなどの手間を加える。まさに日本の粋を存分に味わえる日本食である。

What is Sushi?

Paralleling with tempura and sukiyaki, sushi is an increasingly popular Japanese food all over the world. Its healthy, low-calorie and low-fat nature, and its use of fresh ingredients, including rice, fish, and vegetables, is the reason for its popularity.

Generally speaking, sushi refers to "Edo-mae (Tokyo-style) nigiri-zushi," where rice is mixed with vinegar and salt, and then formed into a rice ball with a slice of fish on top. The history of sushi dates back to the end of the Edo period (at the beginning of the 1800s). As an easy and convenient fast food ordered at street stalls and eaten while standing, sushi was popular among the people of that time.

The craftsmanship of a sushi chef who has served his apprenticeship makes a difference in sushi. The chefs identify seasonal fish, cut it in the most appropriate manner, and spend extra time and effort on pickling, broiling, and simmering it. Sushi is certainly a Japanese food where you can fully enjoy Japanese cultural sophistication.

握り

ワサビをつけた寿司ダネを、手酢を指につけて酢飯を舟形にふんわりと握って成型した、ひと口サイズの寿司。酢飯の分量は寿司ダネによって多少異なるが、だいたい10g前後。握りひとつで1カンと数える。

Nigiri

A single bite-size nigiri is made by a chef who wets his fingers with vinegar and then softly molds the vinegared rice into a boat-shaped rice ball. Although the amount of vinegared rice differs slightly depending on the sushi topping, it is usually about 10 grams per nigiri. One nigiri is counted as 1 kan (a Japanese counting term specifically for sushi).

軍艦巻

ウニやイクラなど、形のくずれやすい寿司ダネを握るときのスタイルで、握った酢飯を海苔で巻き、ワサビをつけて寿司ダネをのせる。横から見た姿が軍艦に似ていることから名づけられた。

Gunkanmaki

(Battleship Roll)

This style holds loose sushi toppings like sea urchin roe (uni) and salmon roe (ikura). The battleship roll is a rice ball with a strip of nori (dried laver seeweed) wrapped around the side, with wasabi on the rice ball and a slice of fish on top. It is called gunkanmaki since it looks like a gunkan (battleship) from the side.

海苔巻

巻き簀にのせた海苔に酢飯を敷き、カンピョウなどの具をのせて巻いた筒状のもの。細巻、中巻、太巻、カッパ巻、鉄火巻など、大きさや材料によって呼び名が変わる。巻き簀で巻かないものは手巻と言う。

Nori-maki

(Rolls with Nori)

Vinegared rice is placed on nori and then topped with ingredients like dried gourd (kanpyo) and everything is rolled up with a maki-su (sushi mat). Nori-maki is a tubular shaped sushi. Depending on the size and ingredients, this type of sushi has different names: hoso-maki (thin roll), chu-maki (medium roll), futo-maki (thick roll), kappa-maki (cucumber roll), and tekka-maki (tuna roll). A sushi roll made without using a maki-su is called te-maki (hand roll).

握り

軍艦巻

海苔巻

寿司の注文の仕方

苦手な寿司ダネやワサビ抜きなどは、注文する前に伝えておく。頼み方は「おまかせ」「お好み」「お決まり」の3種類。好き嫌いがなく、その日の美味しい寿司ダネを味わいたいなら「おまかせ」。予約時に予算を伝えておくと、安心して楽しめる。

好みがはっきりしていて、自分のペースでじっくりと味わいたい人には、寿司ダネを自分で選んで注文する「お好み」がいい。あっさりした寿司ダネから濃厚なものへ進み、玉子や巻物で締めるというのが基本だが、五感を開放させて自由に味わうのが粋。

品書きで値段と内容の検討をつけやすいのが「お決まり」。「松・竹・梅」などのランクがあることが多い。好きなものを追加で握ってもらえば、満足度は一層高まる。

How to Order Sushi

Before ordering, tell your chef if you do not want specific types of fish or wasabi. There are three ways to order sushi: "omakase (chef's choice)," "okonomi (your choice)," and "okimari (set menu)." If you do not have likes or dislikes and would like to enjoy the delicious catch of the day, "omakase" is the way to go. If you mention your budget when making a reservation, you can relax and enjoy your meal.

If you clearly know what you like and want to enjoy eating at your own pace, ordering "okonomi," your choice of sushi, would be best. Although orders usually move from non-fatty to fatty sushi and then finish up with an omelet or roll, unleashing your five senses is a sophisticated way to enjoy sushi uninhibited.

The price and menu content are easily understood when ordering "okimari." The ranks of "matsu (pine), take (bamboo), and ume (plum)" are often used. Order additional sushi as you like for a more fulfilling experience.

寿司の食べ方 箸を使う

How to Eat Sushi with Chopsticks

1

醬油差しから、小皿に適量の醬油を注ぐ。

Pour an adequate amount of soy sauce from the soy sauce cruet into the sauce dish.

4

上側の箸を親指を支点に中指で上下させることで、上手に箸を開閉させることができる。

Move the upper chopstick up and down with the middle finger, using the thumb as a fulcrum. In this way, you can open and close the chopsticks well.

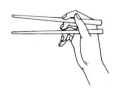

2

下側の箸を薬指と中指の指先の間でつまむようにし、手から1センチほど出るように固定する。

Hold the lower chopstick between the tips of the ring and middle fingers. Fix the chopstick 1 centimeter out of your hand.

3

上側の箸の先を固定した下側にそろえ、中指と人差し指で軽くはさむ。

Make the tip of the upper chopstick even with the lower one. Hold it lightly with the middle and index fingers.

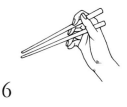

5

寿司を横に倒し、寿司ダネと酢飯が離れないように箸で寿司全体をふんわりとはさむようにする。

Tip over a piece of sushi, and delicately pinch the whole piece with chopsticks in order to keep the sushi topping and vinegared rice together.

6

寿司ダネの先に少量の醤油をつけ、そのまま口に運ぶ。

Dip the tip of the topping into a small amount of soy sauce, and directly transfer the sushi to your mouth.

寿司の食べ方 手を使う

1

寿司を横に倒し、寿司ダネ側に人差し指、中指を添え、親指の3本でやさしくつまみあげる。

Tip over a piece of sushi, and keep the index and middle fingers on the topping side. Place the thumb on the other side, and gently pick up the sushi with those three fingers.

2

寿司ダネの先に少量の醤油をつけ、そのまま口に運ぶ。

Dip the tip of the topping into a small amount of soy sauce, and directly transfer the sushi to your mouth.

How to Eat Sushi with Fingers

14
15

第二章

いろいろな寿司を味わってみよう

Chapter 2
Trying Different
Varieties of Sushi

THE SUSHI
MENU BOOK

鰹

カツオ
KATSUO

Bonita,
skipjack,
ocean bonito
ボニータ、
スキップジャック、
オーシャン・ボニート

KATSUO

旬 From summer to fall

　旬は年2回ある。桜の咲く頃、黒潮にのって姿をみせる春の風物詩が「初ガツオ」。江戸っ子は女房を質に入れてでも食べろと熱狂した。

　初ガツオは赤身が強く、脂は少ないが香り高い。わずかな酸味があり、爽やかな味わいである。

　9月頃に出回るのが「戻りガツオ」。体重が春の倍ほどに増え、脂がのって上質なマグロの中トロにも勝る味。鮮度が落ちやすいので、寿司ダネになったのは昭和に入ってから。串に刺して直火で皮を炙ると、くさみがとれてカツオ特有の芳ばしさが広がる。

　Katsuo is in season twice a year. In spring when cherry blossoms are in bloom, it is common to see the "first katsuo" riding the waves of the Japan Current. A true native of Tokyo would be so excited that he would go so far as to pawn his wife to eat it.

　The meat of the first katsuo is deep red, and although lean, the fish is flavorful. It has a slight acidity and a fresh taste.

　Around September "returning katsuo" appear. The fish has put on fat and weighs twice as much as katsuo found in spring. The returning katsuo has a flavor that is even better than chutoro (medium-fatty tuna). Because it loses freshness easily it wasn't used for sushi until after the Showa Period began in late 1926. When skewered and its skin grilled over a direct flame, the strong smell disappears and the characteristic aroma of katsuo fills the air.

かつお

Katsuo

赤身

Red meat

鮪

マグロ
MAGURO

Tuna
ツナ

MAGURO

旬　冬　Winter

　仕入れたマグロの質で、寿司屋の実力がわかるとも言われる。なかでも本マグロ（クロマグロとも言う）は、まさに寿司ダネの王様。体長3メートル、重さ400キロを超えるものもあり、暖流と寒流が激しくぶつかりあう、青森・大間沖の本マグロは人気が高い。

　甘みと酸味が絶妙な背の部分が赤身（写真後）。腹側のナカ・シモが中トロ（写真中）。たっぷり脂がのっている腹側のカミが大トロ（写真前）。赤身を煮きり醤油に漬けたヅケ、鉄火巻、ネギトロ巻など、さまざまな味わいを楽しめるのが、マグロの醍醐味である。

The proficiency of a sushi restaurant can be distinguished by the quality of the maguro they purchase. Among the types of maguro, the blue-fin tuna (called honmaguro or kuromaguro) is considered the king of sushi.

Some blue-fin grow over 3m in length and weigh more than 400kg. The most popular are caught off the coast of Oma in Aomori, where the warm and cold currents converge in turbulent waters. The exquisite red meat along the back of the maguro (pictured in back) is sweet and acidic. Naka Shimo (the middle and lower portion) is called chutoro (pictured in the middle), and Kami (the fatty meat from the upper belly) becomes otoro (pictured in front). The red meat can be enjoyed in a variety of ways, either marinated in nikiri (zuke), rolled with tuna (tekka-maki), or rolled and topped with tuna and welsh onion (negitoro-maki).

鰈

カレイ
KAREI

Japanese flounder,
flat fish
ジャパニーズ・フランダー、
フラット・フィッシュ

KAREI

旬 Summer

　冬のヒラメが終わると、夏のマコガレイが旬を迎える。透き通るような身が美しい。上品な甘みとほのかな磯の香りが、爽やかな余韻となる。赤身とは違って、奥深さと粋を存分に楽しめる。
　カレイは種類がとても多いが、なかでもマコガレイは、脂ののりが良い高級魚とされている。
　エンガワも忘れてはならない。ヒレの部分の筋肉で、コリコリした食感と脂が舌の上で溶け出し、寿司ダネの中でも一級品。コラーゲンが多く、日本女性のきめ細やかな美肌の秘密が隠されている。

When winter flounder season is over, the summer season is right behind bringing with it marbled flounder. The translucent meat is beautiful, and the delicate sweetness and subtle ocean scent leaves a refreshing feeling. Unlike red meat, white meat has a depth and delicacy that can be fully enjoyed.

There are many types of karei, but the marbled flounder is considered top of the line because of its fatty content.

Engawa, the sinew along the flounder's fin, must not be overlooked. Though it has a tough texture the fatty portion melts on the tongue, and it is one of the prime sushi ingredients. Engawa is rich in collagen and is the secret to Japanese women's beautiful skin tone.

皮剥

カワハギ
KAWAHAGI

File fish,
skinpeeler
ファイルフィッシュ、
スキンピーラー

KAWAHAGI

旬 From summer to fall

　クセのない、あっさりした味わいが魅力。引き締まった歯ごたえのある身が特徴である。

　カワハギの名は、皮をくるりと剥いで料理することに由来している。いかめしい顔つきで、丈夫な歯を持つたくましい魚である。皮はヤスリの代用としても使われるぐらい固い。

　3枚に下ろした切り身を、昆布じめにしたカワハギの握りは美味。さらに、肝をちょんとのせる（写真後）と、また格別の味わいになる。淡白な身に、ねっとりした濃厚な甘みの肝が加わり、底力を感じさせる旨さである。

Kawahagi is appealing because it isn't fishy and has a light flavor. It is known for its firm texture.

The name stems from the fact that it is skinned before preparation. The sturdy fish has a stern-looking face and strong teeth. The skin is so tough that it can be used as an artificial file.

Kawahagi is delicious when sliced and wrapped in konbu, and is even more appetizing when the liver is served on top (pictured in back). The flavor of the simple meat plus the intense sweetness of the soft liver taps an underlying vitality.

間
八

カンパチ
KANPACHI

Allied kingfish,
greater yellowtail
アライドゥキングフィッシュ、
グレーターイエローテール

KANPACHI

 旬 夏　Summer

　眼の上の黒い模様が、上から見ると「八」の字に見えることから名づけられた。関西方面ではアカハナとも言われ、ほんのり桜色に染まった鼻色に由来する。

　養殖が多く、旬の天然物に出合えたら、迷わず握ってもらいたい。少し寝かせると、一段と旨味を増す。「養殖のカンパチでも、ブリよりも味は上」と言われている。

　ブリの仲間だが、ブリよりもあっさりして、くどさが残らない。引き締まった身の歯触りは、刺身にするとより引き立つ。カンパチ独特の甘みは、さらに握ることによって旨味を開花させる。

When viewed from above, the black coloring over the eyes resembles the kanji character for the number 8, thus the Japanese name for kanpachi includes that kanji. In the Kansai area the fish is called akahana (literally, red nose), after the slightly pinkish color of the nose. Kanpachi are often raised on fish farms, so if you happen upon a natural kanpachi when it is in season, don't hesitate to order it. The flavor intensifies if it is set aside for a short time, and it is said that even the kanpachi raised on a fish farm tastes better than buri (yellowtail).

Although related to buri, it has a simpler, lighter taste. The texture of the firm meat becomes even firmer when prepared as sashimi (raw fish), and the sweet flavor characteristic of kanpachi is enhanced when molded into sushi.

鯒

旬 夏　Summer

コチ
KOCHI

Platycephalus indicus
プレイティセファラスインディカス

KOCHI

　旬は夏。頭が大きく黄褐色で見かけは良くないが、身の食感はオコゼにも似た弾力がある高級魚。ほんのりとした甘みには、紅葉おろしも煮きりも両方合う奥深さがある。まさに「夏のフグ」と絶賛される所以である。

　寿司ダネとして使われるようになったのは最近のこと。瀬戸内地方ではガラゴチと呼ばれ、本州中部以南の近海で獲れるので、新鮮なものが入りやすい。5〜8月頃に出回るスズキやホシガレイとは違い、こりこりとした歯ごたえが魅力。身を薄くそぎ落とした握りは、涼を誘い、風を感じさせる爽やかさがある。

Kochi comes into season in summer. Though it lacks visual appeal with its large head and yellowish brown color, it is a highly prized fish whose meat has a springy texture similar to okoze (stingfish) and a hint of sweetness possessing a depth that is suitable served either with grated radish and red pepper, or nikiri . That is precisely why it is praised as the "fugu of summer."

Kochi has only recently been prepared in sushi. In the Setouchi region it is called garagochi, and since it is harvested in the Kinkai area south of central Japan it is easy to obtain fresh fish. In contrast to suzuki (perch) and hoshigarei (spotted halibut), which appear from May to August, its appeal is its tough texture. When thinly sliced, kochi has a freshness that conjures up a cool breeze.

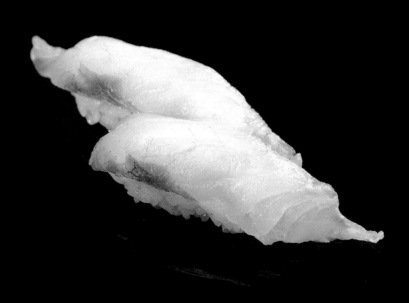

鱸

スズキ
SUZUKI

Perch,
Japanese sea bass
パーチ、
ジャパニーズシーバス

SUZUKI

旬 **夏**　Summer

　その銀色に輝く姿は「タイにも勝る」とも言われる。夏に旬を迎え、春のマダイ、冬のヒラメに匹敵する旨さ。8月半ば頃から、産卵のために味が落ちる。

　背身（写真前）と腹身（写真後）は風味も肉質も、まるで別の魚のような味わい。歯切れの良さを楽しむなら背、脂の甘みを楽しむなら腹身がおすすめ。

　スズキは出世魚。幼魚はコッパ、1年までの25センチくらいのものをセイゴ、2～3年の50センチくらいのものをフッコと呼び、4年以上の60センチほどになった成魚をスズキと言う。大きいものほど美味しい。

This shiny, silver colored fish is said to "beat out even tai (Japanese sea bream)". Suzuki comes into season in summer and has a delicious flavor that rivals summer madai (red sea bream) and winter hirame. From mid-August the flavor suffers due to spawning season.

Meat from the stomach (pictured in back), and backbone (pictured in front), are so different in both taste and quality that it could be from different fish. Meat along the backbone is perfect for those who enjoy a chewy texture, and the belly suits those who prefer the sweetness of a fatty meat.

Suzuki is called by different names as it grows. When a young fry it is called koppa, then seigo when 1 year of age and approximately 25cm, then fukko when 2 to 3 years old and about 50cm. When it reaches 4 years of age and 60cm at adulthood it is called suzuki. The larger the fish, the tastier it is.

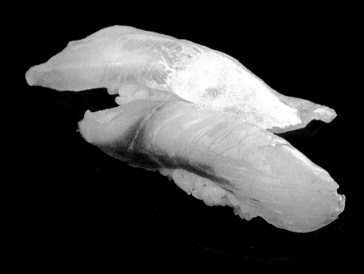

鯛

タイ
TAI

Japanese sea bream,
genuine porgy
ジャパニーズシーブリーム、
ジュニュインポーギー

TAI

旬　**冬～春**　From winter to spring

　日本の祝いの膳には欠かせない、めでたい魚。その姿
形と体色の美しさ、食味の良さから、古代から神前や朝
廷への貢物として奉納された。

　日本で獲れるタイは十数種類ほどあるが、寿司ダネと
して握られるのは「マダイ」。

　タイの握りの楽しみ方は2種ある。皮を引いて奥深い
甘みのある白身本来の味を楽しむものと、皮をつけたま
ま湯引く松皮づくり（写真前）である。松皮づくりは、
職人の技が光る仕事。魚の王様とも称されるタイの皮、
皮下の脂肪、白身と、丸ごと味わうことができる。

Tai is always served at celebratory occasions in Japan. Since ancient
times it has been presented as an offering to the gods or to the
Imperial Court because of its attractive appearance, color, and savory
taste.

There are more than a dozen types of tai harvested in Japan, but
"madai" is used in sushi.

There are 2 ways to enjoy tai, also called king of the fish, either
served skinless to enjoy the concentrated sweet flavor of the white
meat, or as matsukawa-zukuri (pictured in front), parboiled with the
skin. The latter way to serve tai gives the chef a chance to show his
skill and the customer an opportunity to savor the flavor of the entire
fish—the skin, the fat under the skin, and the white meat.

Season　Form　Explanation

平政

ヒラマサ
HIRAMASA

Yellow tail,
amberjack,
goldstriped amberjack
イエローテール、
アンバージャック、
ゴールドストゥライプト
アンバージャック

旬 Summer

　体側に黄色い帯のある形はブリによく似ている。ブリ
より体が平たく細長い。旬は、「冬のブリ、夏のヒラマサ」
と言われ、6月頃から出回る。
　出荷量が少ないために高級魚とされる。ブリに比べる
とさっぱりとした味わい。脂がきつすぎず、非常にバラ
ンスがいい。
　天然のヒラマサは「艶があり、ブリよりも格段に旨い」
と賞する人も多い。その味わいは、じつに複雑。酸味・旨味・
甘みが、絶妙なハーモニーを奏でる。独特の香りと、引
き締まったしなやかな身が舌の上で踊る。

　Similar to buri, hiramasa has a gold band along its body, which is
flatter, longer, and thinner. It comes into season around June. The
saying goes, "buri in winter, hiramasa in summer."
　Because few are caught, it is considered a premium fish. It has a
fresher taste compared to buri, and an extremely fine balance that is
not too fatty.
　Natural hiramasa is prized by many people for being "glossy and
markedly better tasting than buri." That taste is, in fact, complex.
Acidity, umami (savoriness), and sweetness combine for a superb
harmony. The distinctive aroma and lean, delicate, meat create a
symphony on the tongue.

HIRAMASA

平目

ヒラメ
HIRAME

Right eye flounder,
marbled sole
ライトアイフラウンダー、
マーブルソール

HIRAME

旬 　From fall to winter

　真冬に獲れる「寒ビラメ」は、身が引き締まり、噛むと
跳ね返すような力強さがある。透明感あふれる味わいは、
白身魚の王様とも称される。

　醤油をつけても旨いが、香りと甘みを引き出すには、塩
とスダチをのせた握り（写真後）がいい。口に入れた瞬間、
潮風が吹きぬけるような感動を味わえる。

　また、1匹から4本しか取れない貴重なエンガワ（写
真中）（ヒレの筋肉）に出合ったら、迷わず握ってもらおう。

　銚子、三陸、長崎など、全国の近海で獲れるが、なか
でも青森産がもっとも美味と言われている。

　"Kanbirame" is caught in mid-winter. Its meat is so firm that when
bitten into your teeth almost bounce back. Its clean taste gives it the
title, the king of the white meat.

　Hirame is delicious with soy sauce, but salt and Japanese citrus brings
out its aroma and sweetness. The moment you place it in your mouth,
you can almost feel the salty ocean breeze blowing. Never hesitate to
order it for nigiri if you happen upon a coveted engawa (the sinew
along the fin; pictured in the middle). Only four can be had from one
fish.

　Although hirame can be found in the waters around Japan, including
Choshi, Sanriku, and Nagasaki, hirame harvested from Aomori
Prefecture is said to be the most delicious.

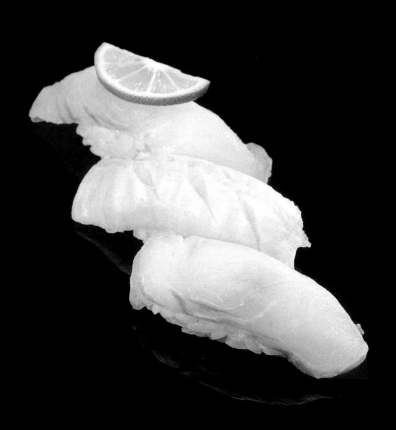

鰤

ブリ
BURI

Yellow tail,
amberjack
イエローテール、
アンバージャック

BURI

旬 冬　Winter

　冬の味覚の代表格。白身の中でももっとも脂がのって甘みが濃く、まるで赤身のような深い味わいを持つ。

　特に真冬に北陸・富山湾の氷見で1本釣りされる「寒ブリ」は絶品。身が締まり、べたついたしつこさが口に残らない。旬の寒ブリの腹側は、マグロの大トロにも匹敵する旨さ。2〜3日熟成させると、さらに旨味を増す。

　ブリは江戸時代（1600-1868年）から庶民に人気の高い魚である。ワカシ→イナダ（ハマチ）→ワラサ→ブリと出世し、体長約1メートルでブリと呼ばれる。体側の黄帯が、英名イエローテールの由来になっている。

　Buri is symbolic of the taste of winter. Among the white meats, it has the most fatty content and the sweetest taste. It has a depth of flavor, just like red meat. In particular, "Kanburi" caught with a single line at Himi in Toyama Bay, Hokuriku are considered outstanding. The meat is firm and there is no persistent tackiness left in the mouth. The belly of seasonal kanburi rivals otoro for taste. The flavor of buri increases when left to mature for 2 to 3 days.

　Buri became popular with the general public in the Edo period (1600–1868). It matures from wakashi, to inada (hamachi), to warasa, to buri, which is approximately 1m in length. The English name yellowtail derives from the gold stripe along the body.

鰺

アジ
AJI

Japanese horse mackerel
ジャパニーズホース
マッカラル

AJI

旬 Summer

　名前は「味」という言葉からきたとも言われ、「あまりに美味しくて参った」と賞賛されたことから「鰺」という字が当てられたという説もある。

　握りで使われるアジと言えばマアジを指す。1年を通じて獲れるが、夏の産卵期がもっとも脂がのって旨い。また、天然のシマアジは、日本近海で獲れる約20種のアジの中でも高級で、繊細な甘みが寿司通をうならせる。

　酢じめは、塩と酢の加減がシンプルなだけに、仕込みの腕が光る寿司ダネ。ワサビと合う。生の握りにはショウガ。新鮮なアジの旨味を一段と引き出す薬味である。

The name is thought to come from the word "aji", which means taste. It is said that the kanji character for aji was given to the fish because it was praised as being "overwhelmingly delicious."

Maaji is used for sushi. Although it can be found year round, the flavor is best in the summer spawning season when fat content is high. In addition, natural shimaaji is the most sought after of the 20 different kinds of aji found in the waters off the shores of Japan. The delicate sweetness is popular with sushi aficionados.

A salt and vinegar marinade is simple, yet reveals the caliber of the sushi chef. It goes will with wasabi, and when served raw, is paired with ginger because it brings out the flavor of fresh aji.

鱚

キス
KISU

Kisu,
sand whiting
キス、
サンドホワイティング

KISU

旬 From spring to summer

　一般にキスと言えばシロギスを指し、古くから寿司ダネとして愛されてきた。春頃から出回り始め、夏の「上寿司ダネ」として寿司通には人気が高い。

　マグロのトロが冬場の旬で脂質が40％であるのに比べ、キスは1％と非常に少ない。いかに淡白か想像できるが、そのあっさりとしたふくよかな旨味がキスの醍醐味。噛むほどに、爽やかな香りが立ちあがる。

　キスの味を、より上品に引き出すのが昆布じめ。皮のほんのり苦い刺激と身の甘みが、舌の上で絶妙に絡み合う瞬間は、まさに至福のときである。

Generally, kisu refers to shirogisu, which has been well-liked as a sushi ingredient since long ago. It appears around springtime and is especially popular with sushi aficionados as "a prime ingredient" for sushi in the summer.

Whereas toro, which comes into season in winter, has a fatty content of 40%, kisu has an extremely low fatty content of 1%. While rather plain, its simple, well-rounded flavor is the best part of kisu. The more it is chewed, the greater the refreshing aroma.

Wrapping it in konbu before serving further draws out the superior quality of its flavor. The moment the ever-so-slightly bitter skin and sweet flavor of the meat meld in your mouth is truly a moment of bliss.

小鰭

コハダ
KOHADA

Gizzard shad
ギザードシャッド

KOHADA

旬 Fall

　銀色の肌がみずみずしく輝く、光り物の王様。江戸前寿司誕生からある定番の寿司ダネで、寿司のためにあるような魚。寿司ダネ以外では、ほとんど使われない。

　3枚に下ろして小骨を丹念にとり、塩を振りきっちり酢でしめる。この仕事ぶりで職人の腕が試される。

　シンコ→コハダ→ナカズミ→コノシロと名前を変える出世魚。シンコは初夏の走りに出回り、小さいので1カンの握りに2〜3匹づけにする。秋になるとコハダが旬を迎える。凛とした姿の美しさ、しっとりとした舌触り、そして上品な甘みが、食べる人の心を震わせる。

　The silver-skin of the kohada glistens. Considered the king of the silver-skinned fish, it has been a staple ingredient used in sushi since Edomae-zushi first appeared. It is almost as if this fish was made for sushi, and in fact, kohada is rarely used in dishes other than sushi.

　Kohada is sliced, the small bones patiently removed, then sprinkled with salt and sufficiently marinated in vinegar. This preparation tests a chef's skill.

　The fish matures from shinko, to kohada, to nakazumi, to konoshiro. Shinko appear in early summer and are small enough that 2 or 3 fish are placed on one serving of sushi. Kohada come into season in fall and has a noble beauty, a delicate texture, and a gentle sweetness that stirs the emotions.

鯖

Season　Form　Explanation

旬 Fall

サバ
SABA

Japanese mackerel,
chub mackerel
ジャパニーズマッカラル、
チャブマッカラル

SABA

　かつては年間100万トンもの水揚げを誇り、身近な食材として日本人に愛され続けてきた魚である。

　秋に旬を迎える。身がまるまると太る秋口のものは秋サバと称され、秋の到来を告げる寿司ダネ。たっぷり脂がのった身をきりりと酢でしめ、しめサバにして握る。口の中で濃厚な脂がじわりと溶ける味わいは格別である。

　寒サバとして絶大な人気の「関サバ」も見のがせない。大分・豊後水道の豊富な餌と、潮の流れで育った驚くほど締まった身。その歯ごたえに感動が走る。

In the past, a million tons of saba were caught yearly, and it continues to be popular with the Japanese people as a familiar part of their meals.

Saba comes into season in fall. Akisaba caught in early fall are plump, and the appearance of saba in sushi heralds the coming of the autumn season. The fully fattened meat is thoroughly soaked in vinegar and prepared as shime-saba (marinated fish). The rich fat slowly melts in your mouth for an exceptional flavor.

The immensely popular "sekisaba" eaten in winter must not be forgotten. The surprisingly firm flesh was fed by the currents and abundant food from the Bungo Channel in Oita, creating an impressive texture.

針魚

サヨリ
SAYORI

Half beak
ハーフビーク

SAYORI

旬 From winter to spring

　春の訪れを告げる江戸前の寿司ダネとして、人々に愛されてきた。群れる習性があり、沢寄りが転じてサヨリと名づけられた。匂いはやや強いが、さっぱりとした初々しい清潔感があり、芯のある余韻が楽しめる。

　細長い体は 40 センチにも成長する。体表は銀色にきらきらと美しく輝く。内蔵を取りのぞき、塩をし、小骨を 1 本 1 本丁寧にぬいていく。下ろした片身 1 本を大胆に 1 カンで食べるのが「輪づくり」（写真後）。サヨリの繊細な美しさに、一層奥ゆかしさを感じさせる。

Sayori has long been loved by the Japanese as an ingredient in Edomae-zushi, and its appearance ushers in the start of spring. The fish swim in groups and were first called sawayori. It has a somewhat strong odor and a fresh, unspoiled simplicity. Sushi lovers enjoy its lingering essence.

The slender fish grows to 40cm and its body is a beautiful, sparkling silver color. The innards are removed, the meat salted, and the small bones are carefully removed one by one. Using an entire piece of filleted sayori for one serving of sushi, called "wazukuri" (pictured on the right), further showcases the delicate beauty of sayori.

白魚

シラウオ
SHIRAUO

Glassfish,
Japanese icefish,
shirauo
グラスフィッシュ、
ジャパニーズ・アイスフィッシュ、
シラウオ

SHIRAUO

旬 From winter to spring

　全長約10センチと細長く、内蔵が見えるほど透明で美しい。湾に棲むことが多く、春先に川をのぼって産卵する。江戸時代は隅田川河口で水揚げされ、江戸前の高級寿司ダネとして珍重された。

　シラウオ漁は、夜ふけにかがり火を焚き、四つ手網ですくう。川面に火がゆらぎ江戸の風物詩であった。近頃は、関西は霞ヶ浦、関東では島根の穴道湖（しんじこ）のものが良いと言われている。

　シラウオは加熱せずに、生のままを握る。普通は軍艦巻で食べるが、江戸前寿司では握りで味わう。つるりとした食感と独特な風味が一度食べたら忘れられない。

This slender fish is about 10cm long, with a beautiful body that is so transparent you can even see its organs. It often lives in bays and in early spring swims upriver to spawn. During the Edo Period it was caught at the mouth of the Sumida River and was highly valued as a premium ingredient in Edo.

The fish are caught in a 4-armed fishing net late at night using beacon lights. Fish from Kasumigaura in the Kansai area and Shinji Lake, Shimane Prefecture in the Kanto area are considered very good.

Shirauo is served raw, without being heated. Usually it is eaten as gunkanmaki but is also enjoyed as nigiri when served Edomae style. Once eaten, the slippery texture and unique flavor are unforgettable.

いくら

イクラ
IKURA

Ikura salmon roe
イクラサーモンロー

IKURA

旬 Fall

　イクラは鮭の卵で、もともとはロシア語の「魚卵」の意味。目の覚めるような深赤色が食欲をそそる。寿司ダネとしての歴史は浅く、ウニと同様、戦後に登場した。

　9月初旬から10月中旬の早い時期のイクラは、皮膜が薄く、なめらかさが格段に上。卵をひとつひとつ丁寧にばらし、醤油・酒などで作った漬け汁に寝かせる。すると一粒一粒の皮膜の中に濃厚な旨味が閉じこめられ、新たな魂が宿る。軍艦巻をほおばるとイクラの粒が弾けて一気に旨味が溢れ出し、酢飯と海苔が味わいを深める。

　イクラは漬け汁に漬けてあるので、食べるときは醤油はつけなくていい。

Ikura is salmon roe and means "fish eggs" in Russian. The eye-popping deep red color stimulates the appetite. It hasn't been used as an ingredient for sushi for long. Just like uni (sea urchin), it was introduced after WWII.

Early in the season from early September until mid-October, ikura have a thin membrane and are dramatically smoother. Each egg is carefully separated and placed in a marinade of ingredients such as soy sauce and rice wine to seal in the rich umami found inside each and every membrane. The ikura topping the gunkanmaki fill your mouth and burst open to instantly release the full flavor, which is enhanced by the vinegared rice and nori.

Ikura are soaked in a marinade so it is not necessary to dip it in soy sauce when eaten.

いくら Ikura 魚卵 Roe

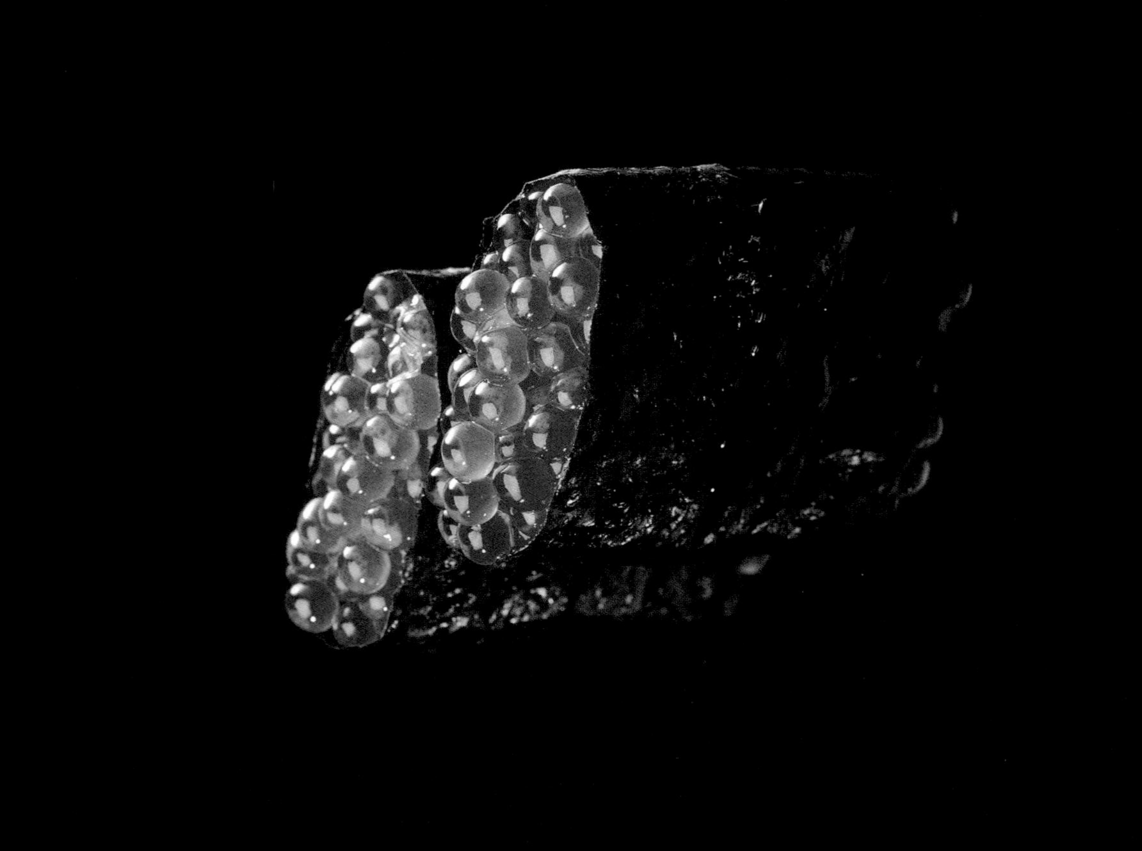

雲丹

ウニ
UNI

Sea urchin
シーアーチン

UNI

旬   From winter to summer

　黄金色の身は、ウニの生殖巣。黄色が強いものを白、赤色が強いものを赤と呼び、赤のほうが甘みが強い。

　日本近海に 180 種類ほど生息し、食べられるのは 10 種類前後。寿司ダネとしては、ムラサキウニ、バフンウニが使われることが多い。

　西日本ではアカウニが有名だが、もっとも上等と言われるのが、北海道と東北で獲れるエゾバフンウニである。粒が小さめで張りがあり、濃いオレンジ色が特徴。口に入れた瞬間、濃厚な甘みがいっぱいに広がる。軍艦巻が一般的だが、握るとウニ独特の磯の香りが引き立つ。

This golden-colored delicacy is actually the sea urchin's gonads. Uni that is primarily yellowish in color is called white uni, and those primarily reddish in color are called red uni and have a much sweeter flavor.

There are as many as 180 different species in the waters near Japan, but only 10 or so can be eaten. Murasakiuni and bafununi are the most common types used in sushi.

Akauni is well-known in western Japan, but the best uni is said to be ezobafununi, harvested in Hokkaido and northeastern Japan. The grains are small, springy, and characteristically deep orange in color. The moment it is placed in your mouth the rich sweetness fills your senses. It is generally served as gunkanmaki, but preparing it as nigiri draws out its distinctive aroma reminiscent of the seashore.

数
の子

カズノコ
KAZUNOKO

Herring roe
ヘリングロー

旬 Spring

　ニシンの卵を塩漬けにしたものがカズノコ。黄金色に輝く粒から、別名を黄色いダイヤとも言う。丹念に塩ぬきすると、磯の香りがふんわり広がって酢飯に合う。ひと腹の卵の多さは、魚の中でも随一。卵がいっせいに口の中で弾け、こりこりした歯ごたえは、他に類がない。

　ニシンが昆布に卵を産みつけた子持ち昆布も、カズノコ同様、小気味いい歯ごたえが絶品。

　３月頃から、ニシンは産卵のために、北海道沿岸に押し寄せる。この新物の「春カズノコ」は、地元北海道以外では、なかなか味わえない希少な一品。

Kazunoko are herring roe that have been pickled in salt. It is also known as yellow diamonds, so named for the shiny, golden-colored grains. Thoroughly washing away the salt gently brings out the smell of the sea and goes well with vinegared rice. Kazunoko has the greatest number of eggs found in one fish. The roe burst open at once in your mouth and the crispy texture is second to none.

Herring lay their eggs on konbu, and just like kazunoko, komochi konbu is prized for its gratifyingly crunchy texture.

Around March, herring rush to the shores of Hokkaido to spawn. These fresh "spring kazunoko" are a rare delicacy outside of Hokkaido.

KAZUNOKO

青柳

アオヤギ
AOYAGI

Japanese orange clam,
hen clam
ジャパニーズ・オレンジ・
クラム、
ヘン・クラム

AOYAGI

旬 冬〜春   From winter to spring

　正式名称はバカガイ。朱色の舌をだらりとだらしなく出した姿にその名が由来する。ハマグリに似た丸みのある殻を開くと、見事なオレンジ色の足が姿を現す。軽く包丁でたたき、湯引きしてから握る。

　アオヤギの貝柱は「小柱」と言われ、アオヤギ（写真前）よりも値が張り、親バカとも言われる。小柱は、寿司ダネでも人気の握りのひとつで、大きいものを大ボシ（写真中）、小さいものは小ボシと呼ばれる。

　小ボシをたっぷりと軍艦巻（写真後）にのせ、その凝縮された旨味を、歯ごたえと共に食べるのが贅沢な味わい方。

　The proper name for this shellfish is bakagai, but the name aoyagi comes from the shape of the scarlet colored tongue that loosely hangs out. When the round shell resembling hamaguri is opened, the intensely orange-colored legs are visible. It is used for sushi topping after lightly cracking it with a knife and parboiling.

　The eye of the aoyagi is called "kobashira" and is more expensive than aoyagi (pictured in front), a somewhat silly situation. Kobashira is also quite popular as a sushi ingredient. Larger ones are called oboshi (pictured in the middle) and smaller ones koboshi. Serving a generous amount of koboshi on gunkanmaki (pictured in back) is an extravagant way to enjoy the concentrated umami and texture.

赤貝

アカガイ
AKAGAI

Bloody clam,
ark shell
ブラッディ・クラム、
アーク・シェル

AKAGAI

旬 冬〜春　　From winter to spring

　身が赤いことからアカガイと名づけられ、江戸前寿司の始めからある基本の寿司ダネ。普通は貝の血液は緑色だがアカガイの血は赤いため、鮮やかな色をしている。アカガイ特有の香り、渋みのある甘み、なめらかな舌触りは、貝の寿司ダネの中でも一番人気。

　アカガイを注文すると、パンッとまな板に叩きつける小気味いい音が聞こえてくる。身がきゅっとしまり、切れ目の入った貝がゆっくり広がり、見事な花を咲かせる。歯ごたえのある「ヒモ（写真後）」は、アカガイよりも旨いと熱狂する人もいるほどである。

　The name akagai (literally, red shell) stems from the red color of the body. This shellfish has been a staple sushi ingredient since Edomae-zushi came into existence. Usually shellfish blood is green, but akagai's red blood gives its vivid color. It is the most popular shellfish used as sushi topping due to its unique aroma, astringent sweetness, and the smooth, pleasant sensation it has on the tongue.

　If you order akagai, you will hear the pleasing sound of the shellfish striking the cutting board, which tightens the flesh. The shellfish is sliced to slowly open, as if a magnificent flower were blooming. There are some who enthusiastically claim that the crunchy "himo (mantle; pictured in back)" tastes even better than the akagai itself.

鮑

アワビ
AWABI

Abalone
アバロン

AWABI

旬 夏〜秋　　From summer to fall

　昆布をたっぷり食べて、海の恵みが丸ごと凝縮された
アワビ。コリコリとはね返してくる力強い歯ごたえと、
ふくよかな磯の香りに魅了される。上物は、青黒色のク
ロアワビと言われ、寿司ダネの中でもかなり高価。
　アワビは、不老不死の妙薬とも言われるコンドロイチ
ンを多く含み、噛むたびに滲み出る繊細な甘みに底力を
感じさせる。
　生（右写真）が持つ歯ごたえも捨てがたいが、旨味が
増す「蒸しアワビ」や、江戸前では夏の煮ダネとして欠
かせない「煮アワビ」の握りも格別。また、ポン酢で食
すワタも、独特の滋味があっておすすめ。

Awabi feeds on an abundance of konbu and is full of the blessings
of the sea. It has a springy, crunchy texture and is filled with the
aroma of the sea. The bluish black kuroawabi is considered high in
quality and is one of the higher priced sushi ingredients.

Awabi contains a high concentration of the health remedy,
chondroitin. Each time it is bitten into its delicate sweetness is
released, tapping into an undercurrent of energy.

While the tough texture of raw awabi (pictured at right) can't be
dismissed, steaming awabi increases its umami, and sushi made with
"mushiawabi (simmered awabi)", Edomae-style, has an exceptional
flavor that is not to be missed in summertime. Wata (intestines) eaten
with ponzu sauce is also recommended for its unique savory flavor.

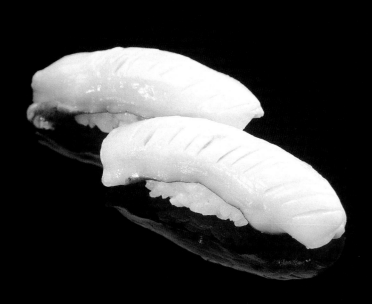

平貝

タイラガイ
TAIRAGAI

Japanese pen shell
ジャパニーズ・
ペン・シェル

旬 Spring

　内湾の砂泥底に棲み、成長すると殻が長さ 30 センチにもなる。大ぶりなものほど味が良い。かつては東京湾でも獲れたが、広く東南アジアまで分布し、特に瀬戸内海や有明海に多い。

　正式名称をタイラギと言うが、ヒモやワタなど、貝柱以外は泥臭くて食べられない。そのため貝柱の部分をタイラガイと呼んでいる。

　甘みはホタテにはかなわないが、しこしことした歯ごたえや旨味ではタイラガイも負けてはいない。生も良いが、少し厚めに切って炙るとぐっと甘みが出る。醤油より塩で味わうと、素材そのものの味が引き立つ。

Tairagai live in the sandy bottom of bays. Its shell reaches up to 30cm when fully grown, and the larger the shellfish, the better the taste. In the past it was harvested from Tokyo Bay, but is found as far as southeast Asia. It is especially abundant in the Seto Inland Sea and Sea of Ariake. Its proper name is dairagi. Except for kaibashira, parts such as himo and wata are inedible due to the smell of mud, therefore kaibashira is called tairagai.

Though tairagai doesn't match the sweetness of hotate (scallops), its firm texture and umami can't be beat. Tairagai tastes good eaten raw, but its sweet flavor is enhanced when sliced somewhat thickly and grilled. Serving it with salt rather than soy sauce draws out the pure flavor of the shellfish.

TAIRAGAI

鳥貝

トリガイ
TORIGAI

Japanese cockle
ジャパニーズコックル

旬 From fall to winter

　殻の大きさは 10 センチほど。食べるのは紫黒色をした足の部分。この形が鳥のくちばしに似ていることから名づけられた。別の説では、鶏肉と味が似ているからとも言われている。

　墨の色が美しいものほど、鮮度がいい。身が厚いものは味が良く、春の時期が一段と美味しい。

　身がふんわりと柔らかく、トリガイ独特の甘みが貝ファンを魅了する。貝類の中でもっとも旨いと評する人もいるほどである。.

　新鮮な上物は、どの寿司ダネにも引けをとらない。

The shell is approximately 10cm. The edible portion is the purplish black legs, which resemble a bird's beak, hence the name torigai (literally, bird shell). Another theory says it received its name because it tastes like chicken.

The more attractive the ink color, the fresher it is. The thick-bodied torigai are flavorful, and the taste is even better in spring.

The meat is light and soft, and its characteristic sweetness appeals to shellfish lovers. There are those who believe torigai is the most flavorful of all shellfish. Fresh, premium torigai favorably compare with any other sushi ingredients.

TORIGAI

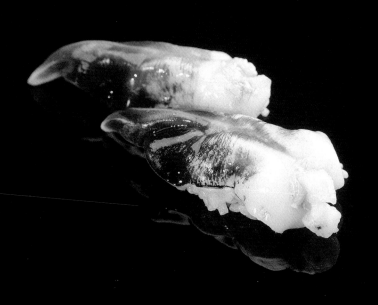

蛤

ハマグリ
HAMAGURI

Hard clam
ハード・クラム

旬 Winter

　平安時代の貝合わせ、桃の節句の潮汁など、1万年前の貝塚から殻がみつかるほど、日本人とハマグリとの関係は古い。東京湾ではかつて山のように獲れ、今でも江戸前寿司には欠かせない寿司ダネである。

　酒蒸しするか、サッと茹でてから、砂糖・みりん・醤油などを合わせた煮汁に漬けこむ。この一連の仕込みは、ハマグリ本来が持つやさしさに強烈な力強さを与える。その煮汁を煮つめたものが煮ツメ。この煮ツメを寿司ダネの上にとろりと塗ると、ハマグリの旨味を際立たせ、酢飯と出合って見事な調和をなす。

Japanese people have a long history with hamaguri. It was used in a shell-matching game in the Heian Period, is eaten in a soup during the Momo no Sekku Festival, and was even found in piles of shells dating from 10,000 years ago. It was once harvested in abundance from Tokyo Bay, and even today is a fundamental ingredient in Edomae-zushi.

Its gentle flavor intensifies when either seasoned with salt and sake then steamed (sakamushi), or lightly boiled then marinated in a broth of ingredients such as sugar, mirin, and soy sauce, resulting in a broth concentrate called nitsume that is thickly brushed on the sushi to accentuate the umami. The combination with vinegared rice makes for an excellent balance.

HAMAGURI

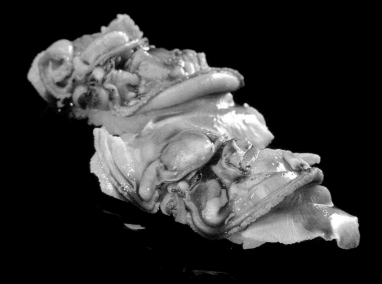

Hamaguri

[1]

Shellfish

帆立貝

ホタテガイ
HOTATEGAI

Scallop
スカラップ

旬 Winter

　冷たい北の海を好み、3年で成熟し直径10センチほどに育った貝の貝柱が食べ頃。形が大きいものほど旨い。

　グリコーゲンを多く含み、生で食べる二枚貝の中ではもっとも甘みが強い。太く大きい貝柱の繊維を楽しむため、少し厚めに切って握られる。ホタテガイが、酢飯をふわりと包みこみ、ふくよかな甘みが広がる。

　江戸前寿司では、醤油や酒などで丸ごとこっくりと煮こむ寿司ダネも定番。店によって味の個性が異なり、生と煮ホタテでは驚くほど違った表情を見せる。両方とも贅沢に味わいたい握りである。

Hotategai is partial to the cold northern sea. It takes 3 years to mature, and is ripe for eating when the kobashira reaches a diameter of 10cm. The larger the hotategai, the better the flavor.

It contains an abundance of glycogen and has the sweetest flavor among clams that are eaten raw. To enjoy the large, fat kobashira they are thickly sliced and then molded into sushi. The hotategai gently envelops the vinegared rice and the heavy, sweet flavor diffuses in your mouth.

In Edomae-zushi, it is standard to simmer the entire shellfish in soy sauce or sake. The flavor differs with each restaurant. The presentation of raw and simmered clams is surprisingly different, but both are sumptuous ways to enjoy hotategai.

北寄貝

ホッキガイ
HOKKIGAI

Surf clam
サーフ・クラム

旬 From winter to spring

　貝に刻まれた線は、成長した1年ごとの年輪である。正式名称はウバガイ、大きいものほど味は良い。殻から取り出し、足の部分を食べる。

　東北や北海道にのみ生息し、ホッキと言われた。輸送技術が進歩した今、ホッキガイとして全国的に寿司ダネとして使われている。生食もあるが、灰色か紫褐色の身をさっと熱湯にくぐらせると、美しい桃色へと変わる。

　よく比較されるのがアカガイ。香りではかなわないが、甘みと旨味はホッキガイのほうが強い。柔らかい身は、噛むほどに滋味が滲み出る。

Each line etched on the shellfish marks one year of growth. Its true name is ubagai, and the larger the shellfish the better the taste. The meat is removed from the shell and the legs are eaten.

Hokkigai only inhabits northeastern Japan and Hokkaido, where it is called hokki, but with advanced modes of transportation it is now used in sushi nationwide as hokkigai. It can be eaten raw, but when the grayish or purplish brown meat is dipped in boiling water, it turns a beautiful peachy color.

Hokkigai is often compared to akagai and though not as fragrant, hokkigai is sweeter and more flavorful. Each time the soft meat is chewed, its flavor is released.

海松貝

ミルガイ
MIRUGAI

Shell siphon,
giant clam,
keen's gaper
シェルサイフォン、
ジャイアントクラム、
キーンゲイパー

MIRUGAI

旬 冬　Winter

　海松（みる）という海藻が殻に生えていることから、この名前がつけられた。殻から伸びた太く大きな水管の部分が、寿司ダネになる。熱湯にさっとくぐらせ、黒い薄皮を剥がすと、琥珀色の身が姿を現す。

　殻の色が黒いものほど新鮮。時間が経つと柔らかくなるので、ミルガイの良さを味わうには鮮度が命。こりこりとした歯ごたえはアワビに勝るとも劣らず、貝類の中ではトップクラスである。

　かつては貝の宝庫だった東京湾でも獲れたが、今は全国的に水揚げが少ないため、高価な寿司ダネである。

The name mirugai comes from the seaweed called miru that grows on the shell. The large, thick valve protruding from the shell is the portion used in sushi. It is dipped in boiling water and the dark, thin skin is removed to reveal the golden brown meat.

The darker the shell, the fresher the shellfish. Mirugai becomes softer as time passes, so freshness is of utmost importance if the flavor of mirugai is to be fully enjoyed. It is just as crunchy as awabi and is considered premium shellfish.

Mirugai was once harvested from Tokyo Bay when the waters were rich with shellfish, but these days it has become a pricey sushi ingredient because there are few places it is harvested in Japan.

穴子

アナゴ
ANAGO

Conger sea eel,
Japanese conger
コンガーシーイール、
ジャパニーズコンガー

ANAGO

旬 　Summer

　ウナギ型の体形で、１メートルほどある。砂地の中に
も棲むが、岩穴にいることから名づけられた。煮物の寿
司ダネの代表で、江戸前寿司の醍醐味が凝縮されている。
　６月からが最盛期。「梅雨時のアナゴは絶品」と昔から
称される。
　脂肪分はウナギの半分ほどしかないが、淡白な白身を
じっくり煮ると、旨味のつまった黄色い脂が皮の表面に
たっぷりと浮かびあがる。仕上げは、煮込んで煮汁をつ
くる甘辛いツメ。こっくりと塗ると、アナゴの旨さが何
倍にもふくらんで、その本領を発揮する。

Anago is similar in length to unagi and grows up to 1m in length.
It lives in sandy soil but gets it name from living in caverns (called
iwaana). Anago is the perfect example of a simmered sushi ingredient
and epitomizes Edomae-zushi.

It reaches its peak from June. It has long ago been said that "anago
during the rainy season is a superb delicacy".

Anago has only half the fatty content of unagi but when the simple
white meat is thoroughly simmered, the yellowish fat filled with
savory flavor floats to the surface of the skin. Before serving, it is
generously topped with the salty-sweet tsume sauce it was simmered
in to increase the delicious flavor many times over and fully showcase
its qualities.

烏
賊

イカ
IKA

Big fin reef squid
ビッグ・フィン・リーフ
スクイッド

IKA

旬 　Summer

　日本人は無類のイカ好き。世界で消費される約40%を占めている。日本近海で獲れるイカは約100種類ほど。寿司ダネとしては、アオリイカ、スミイカ、ヤリイカ、ホタルイカなどがある。

　なかでも、夏に旬を迎えるアオリイカの人気は高い。ねっとりと舌に絡む深い甘みは、酢飯との相性が抜群。身が透明なのでミズイカとも言われ、最高級とされる。歯ごたえが良いゲソの握り（写真後）も旨い。

　ヤリイカは春イカとも言われ、身が薄く繊細な甘みがあり、スミイカは、肉厚な身と歯触りが身上である。

　Japanese people love excellent ika and consume about 40% of the squid worldwide. Approximately 100 different kinds of ika are caught in the waters off the Japan coast, and aoriika, sumiika, yariika, and hotaruika among others are used in sushi.

　The most popular is aoriika, which comes into season in summer. It has a rich sweetness that adheres to the tongue and is exceptionally compatible with vinegared rice. It is also called mizuika because of its translucent body and it is considered a choice ingredient for sushi. The crunchy geso (tentacles; pictured on the right) are also flavorful.

　Yariika is also known as spring ika and is thin with a subtle sweetness, while sumiika has thick meat and a very nice chewy texture.

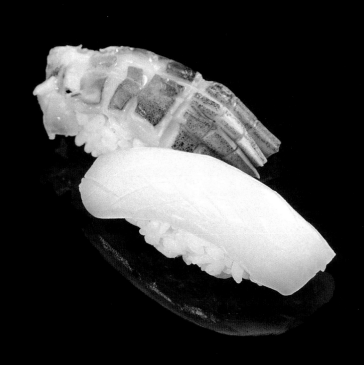

海老

エビ
EBI

Kuruma prawn,
tiger prawn
クルマ・プラウン ,
タイガー・プラウン

EBI

旬 Summer

　長いヒゲと曲がった腰から「海老」の字が当てられ、長寿を象徴する縁起物。寿司ダネとしてよく使われるのは、体長 20 センチほどのクルマエビ。出世魚のように、小さいものからサイマキ、マキ、クルマエビ、大車（おおぐるま）と名前を変える。

　江戸前寿司では、曲がらないよう串に刺して茹であげたもの（写真後）を酢にひたすと、艶やかな朱色になる。

　生（写真前）のまま握る「おどり」も、エビの醍醐味。また、日本特産種の肉厚なボタンエビは、口の中でとろりと溶ける極上の甘みを堪能できる。

The characters for ebi ('sea' and 'old') are used because of its long beard and curved back. Ebi is thought to symbolize longevity.

Kurumaebi are about 20cm in length and often used in sushi. Just like fish that go by different names as they mature, as ebi grows it is called saimaki, maki, kurumaebi, and then oguruma.

In Edomae-zushi, ebi is prepared by straightening it on a skewer, boiling it (pictured in back), and then dipping the ebi in vinegar to create a lovely vermillion color.

Preparing it raw (pictured in front) as "odori" is another way to fully enjoy ebi.

Botanebi is a type of ebi produced in Japan that has fleshier meat. Its exquisite sweet flavor deliciously melts in your mouth for a thoroughly enjoyable experience.

蝦蛄

シャコ
SHAKO

Mantis shrimp,
squilla
マンティスシュリンプ、
スキラ

SHAKO

旬 　From spring to summer

　体長15センチほど。エビとカニの両方の旨味を閉じ込めたような味わいが魅力。灰色の体表は茹でるとシャクナゲ色に変わり、転じてシャコとなったと言われる。ほくほくした身に奥深い甘みがあり、煮汁を煮つめた濃厚なツメが塗られる。

　晩秋の脱皮前も旬であるが、春先から初夏にかけて獲れる子持ちシャコが最上とされる。カツブシと呼ばれる卵は絶品。また、はさみの肉「つめ」は歯ごたえが良く甘みが濃厚。1匹のシャコから、たった二つしか取れないものを軍艦巻で供される。

Shako is approximately 15cm in length. Its appeal lies in the fact that its flavor seems to have sealed in both the umami of ebi and kani (crab). When boiled, its gray appearance turns the color of rhododendrons (shakunage), which is why it is called shako. The firm meat has a rich, sweet flavor and is served brushed with a concentrated tsume sauce.

It comes into season in late fall before molting, but shako carrying eggs, which appear from early spring to early summer, are considered the best. The roe, called katsubushi, is a top grade delicacy.

Meat from "tsume (the pincers)" is crunchy and quite sweet. Only 2 can be had from one shako, and they are served as a topping on gunkanmaki.

蛸

タコ
TAKO

Common octpus
コモン・オクトパス

TAKO

旬 From summer to fall

　寿司ダネによく使われるマダコは、夏と秋の２回、旬がある。マダコの中でも「立って歩く」と言われる明石産が絶品。身が締まり、噛むほどに旨味が滲み出る。特に味が充実してくるのは、体重２〜３キロほどに成長したものと言われる。

　番茶で茹でた「ゆでダコ（右写真）」は旨味が凝縮され、しっとりした柔らかな身に様変わり。酢飯との相性も良い。また、薄造りにして握った「生ダコ」は、醤油よりも塩が美味。タコの甘みがぐっと引き出され、スダチをしぼると爽やかな香りと味が広がる。

Madako is often used as a sushi topping and comes into season twice a year, in summer and fall. Madako from Akashi "walks upright" and is considered the best. Its meat is firm, and the more it is bitten into, the more umami that is released. Those that have reached 2–3 kilos in weight are regarded as especially delicious.

Boiling it in coarse green tea, "yudedako" (pictured at right) condenses the savory flavor and completely transforms the meat into a soft delicacy. It goes well with vinegared rice.

Thinly sliced "namadako (raw tako) " is also used as sushi topping, and tastes better with salt than soy sauce because it draws out the tako's sweet flavor. Serving it with sudachi (Japanese citrus) increases the refreshing fragrance and flavor.

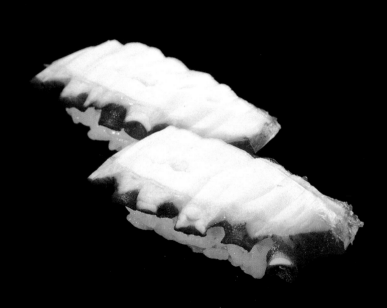

玉子焼き

タマゴヤキ
TAMAGOYAKI

Japanese-style
chunky omelet
ジャパニーズスタイル
チャンキーオムレツ

旬 **通年** Year round

　黄色が目に眩しいふっくら焼きあがった玉子焼きは、昔から「玉子で始まり玉子で終わる」と言われるほど、それぞれの寿司屋の特色が出るネタである。

　玉子焼きは、大きく分けると２種類。ひとつは、「コミ」（右写真）と言われる芝エビや白身のすり身、ヤマトイモなどを混ぜて作る「カステラ風の玉子焼き」。上品な洋菓子のような口溶けで、玉子とコミの奥深い甘みは、驚きの美味しさである。もうひとつが、カツオだしをきかせた「だし巻玉子」。玉子にぎゅっとだしの旨味が凝縮し、酢飯との相性も抜群である。

Tamagoyaki is a type of light, fried omelette that is bright yellow in color. Since long ago each sushi restaurant has had its own distinctive tamagoyaki dish, and in fact there is even a saying, "begin with egg and end with egg."

Generally, there are two types of tamagoyaki. One is called "komi" (pictured at right) and includes ingredients such as prawns, ground white fish meat, and Japanese potato to create a "cake-like tamagoyaki". It melts in the mouth like a superbly created cake, and the rich sweetness of the egg and komi is surprisingly delicious. Another type, called "dashimaki tamago", is seasoned with katsuo dashi soup stock. The flavor of the dashi is concentrated in the egg, and it is a perfect match to vinegared rice.

TAMAGOYAKI

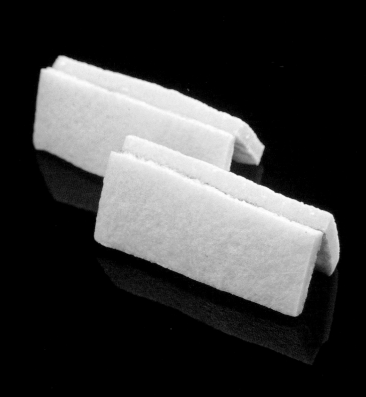

ば
らちらし

バラチラシ
BARA-CHIRASHI

旬 Year round

　新鮮な魚介と、さまざまな具材がひとつの器の中でみごとに融合する極上の一品。寿司ダネが握りとはまったく違った表情をみせ、何種類もの味をいっぺんに楽しむことができる。

　具材は、細かく切った魚介類や、玉子、甘辛く煮た椎茸、カンピョウ、おぼろなど。彩りが華やかで、目にも美味しい。

　ちらしとは、もともとは具と酢飯を混ぜ合わせたものを「五目」、上に散らしたものを「ちらし」と呼ばれていた。

　小皿に入れた醤油を上から少量たらすか、寿司ダネに醤油をつけながら食べる。

 Fresh seafood and various ingredients are combined in one bowl to create an exceptional dish. It is an entirely different presentation than molded sushi, but a variety of different flavors can be enjoyed at once.

 Ingredients include finely chopped seafood, egg, shiitake mushrooms simmered in a salty sweet sauce, kanpyo, and shredded kelp. Bara-chirashi is a colorful dish that looks delicious.

 Originally, "chirashi" referred to ingredients sprinkled on top of "gomoku", vinegared rice mixed with various foods. A little soy sauce is sprinkled from a small plate over the chirashi or the sushi toppings are dipped in soy sauce as they are eaten.

鉄火丼

テッカドン
TEKKA-DON

旬 **通年** Year round

　鮮やかな色のマグロが、丼いっぱいに覆いつくされ、マグロを思う存分に堪能できる。適宜醤油をつけながら食すものと、醤油・みりんなどに漬けたヅケマグロを使ったものもある。

　鉄火の名は、幕末から明治の初頭に、鉄火場（バクチ場）に届けさせた出前寿司に由来する。当時の巻物とは、カンピョウ巻のことを指すが、変わった寿司を鉄火場の衆が頼み、手に飯粒のつかないマグロの巻物・鉄火巻（→P90）が誕生し、これを丼にしたもの。

This dish consists of a bowl of rice generously covered with brightly colored maguro, so you can eat your fill of the fish. It is either served with soy sauce that you can add as you like, or with zukemaguro that has already been marinated in seasonings such as soy sauce and mirin.

The name tekka comes from sushi that was delivered to the tekka-ba (bakuchijo, gaming rooms) from the end of the Edo Period to the start of the Meiji Period. At that time, rolled sushi referred to kanpyo-maki, but at the request of the people at the bakuchijo for a different kind of sushi, tekka-maki (maguro-roll; see pg. 90) were created as sushi that wouldn't leave hands sticky with rice.

細巻

ホソマキ
HOSO-MAKI

旬 Year round

① ［ねぎトロ巻］脂ののったマグロの中落ちを削いだ身と、小ネギの海苔巻。削ぎ取ることを「ねぎる」と言う。

② ［かっぱ巻］キュウリの海苔巻。カッパは水の神様とも言われ、江戸時代は初物を川に流してお供えした。

③ ［穴きゅう巻］煮アナゴとキュウリの海苔巻。

④ ［カンピョウ巻］ウリ科ユウガオの実を紐状にむいて乾燥させ、それを水でもどして甘辛く煮る。江戸前寿司の代表的な海苔巻。

⑤ ［紐きゅう巻］アカガイの紐とキュウリの海苔巻。

⑥ ［鉄火巻］マグロの赤身の海苔巻。鉄火場で手づかみで食べたことに由来するとも言われる。

① **Negi-toro-maki:** Nori-maki with flaked fatty tuna meat from between the ribs and green onion. "Negiru" means to shave off the tuna meat.

② **Kappa-maki:** Nori-maki with cucumber. Since kappa (river sprites) were considered water gods, the first cucumbers of the season were thrown into the river as offerings during the Edo period.

③ **Ana-kyu-maki:** Nori-maki with cooked anago and cucumber.

④ **Kanpyo-maki:** Strands of peeled and dried bottle gourd simmered in sugar and soy sauce. It is a typical Edomae-zushi nori-maki (various ingredients rolled in vinegared rice and wrapped in a sheet of nori).

⑤ **Himo-kyu-maki:** Nori-maki with akagai mantle and cucumber.

⑥ **Tekka-maki:** Nori-maki with red tuna meat. So named because it was eaten by hand at gaming rooms (tekka-ba).

太巻

フトマキ
FUTO-MAKI

旬 通年　Year round

　海苔2枚を大胆に使い、寿司飯をたっぷりとのせる。具材は、アナゴ、かんぴょう、イカ、エビ、玉子など、山の幸から海の幸までを一挙に巻きこむ百花繚乱。彩り鮮やかな豪華さは、まさに圧巻。

　店によって、また季節によって具材は異なり、まったく違った味わいを楽しめるのも、太巻きならではの魅力である。

　食べごたえのあるずっしりとした重量感が腹を満たし、やさしい甘さ、深い旨味、歯ごたえなど、寿司の醍醐味のすべてが1本につまっている。

Futo-maki generously uses two sheets of nori to hold a good amount of vinegared rice. With anago, kanpyo, squid, shrimp, and omelet as fillings, a futo-maki wraps together every goodness of the land and the sea. Futo-maki with absolutely gorgeous vivid colors is truly a masterpiece.

Depending on the sushi bar or the season, the fillings are different. The fact that futo-maki, unlike other sushi, can be made with completely different flavors is appealing.

The filling and hearty futo-maki satisfies your appetite. A slight sweetness, intricate flavors, and pleasant textures… everything appealing about sushi is packed into a roll of futo-maki.

FUTO-MAKI

珍味

チンミ
CHINMI

このわた
KONOWATA

Salted Entrails of Trepang (Sea Cucumber)

ナマコからほんのわずかしかとれない
腸を、塩漬けした珍味。上質なものは
琥珀色に輝き、酒好きをうならせる。

Konowata is a delicacy made of salted sea
cucumber intestines. Each sea cucumber only
has a small amount of intestines. High quality
konowata has an amber glow and is appreciated
by sake lovers.

からすみ
KARASUMI

Dried Mullet Roe

ボラの卵を塩漬けして干し固めた、高価
な珍味。10月頃に仕込む。旨味が濃縮さ
れ、酒の肴として人気が高い。

Karasumi is an expensive delicacy of striped
mullet roe that has been pickled and dried. It
is prepared around October. The flavor is so
intense that dried mullet roe is popular as an
appetizer consumed with sake.

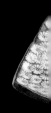

さざえの壷焼き
SAZAE-NO-TSUBOYAKI

Turban Snail Cooked in the Shell

殻の中でたっぷり滋味が煮つまった汁がぐつぐつと音を立て、サザエを丸ごと味わう一品。身は柔らかく、スープは絶品。

This is a dish to enjoy the whole goodness of the turban snail shimmering down to the nutrient-rich juice inside. The meat is tender, and the juice is exquisite.

海老の
塩焼き
EBI-NO-SIOYAKI

Broiled Shrimp with Salt

塩を振り、殻ごとカリッと炙る。ミソのつまった頭も格別。皮を剥ぐと、蒸し焼きされた身から、ふんわり甘い香りが立ちのぼる。

Unshelled shrimp is crisply broiled with a sprinkling of salt. The head of the shrimp contains a rich filling that is exceptionally good. When unshelled, a sweet flavor gently wafts up from the steamed meat.

煮物

ニモノ
NIMONO

煮いか
NI-IKA

Simmered Squid

あっさりと煮たヤリイカの身に、酢飯
がつめられている。甘めの煮ツメがぬ
られていて、外国人に人気。

Sushi rice is stuffed in a simply cooked squid
that is basted with sweet nitsume. This dish is
popular with international audiences.

鯛の兜煮
TAI-NO-KABUTO-NI

Simmered Helmet
(Simmered Japanese Sea Bream Head)

濃厚な味わいのタイの頭を、醤油、砂糖、
酒などで煮る。目玉のゼラチン質がと

茶碗蒸し
CHAWAN-MUSHI

Savory Steamed Egg Custard

エビや銀杏などの具を入れ、卵とだし
汁でつくる寿司店の隠れた名脇役。な
めらかな舌触りが魅力。夏場に冷やし
て食べるのも格別。

This savory steamed egg custard is made from
eggs and soup stock and garnished with shrimp
and ginko nuts. It holds a secondary status but
is a staple at the sushi bar. Its velvety feeling
on the palate is irresistible, and it is also great
served cold in the summer.

蒸し鮑
MUSHI-AWABI

Steamed Abalone

正確には酒煮。煮ることによって、旨
味がぎゅっと凝縮される。ムチムチし
た食感は絶品。ワサビ醤油で食べても
いい。

Abalone should be simmered with sake.
Simmering allows the flavors to condense. Its
resilient texture is superb. It is also enjoyable
eaten with soy sauce seasoned with wasabi.

野菜

季節の野菜
KISETSU-NO-YASAI

Seasonal Vegetables

クサソテツの一瞬の芽吹きを味わう春の山菜「こごみ」や、春の訪れを告げる「たけのこ」など、自然の恵みを盛り込んだ一品。旬の野菜を、存分に味わえる贅沢なつまみ。

Seasonal vegetables are filled with the blessings of nature, including an edible wild plant in the spring called "kogomi", the sprout of matteuccia struthiopteris that we can enjoy only for a short period of time, and "takenoko (bamboo shoot)" which marks the beginning of spring. The flavor of seasonal vegetables can be fully enjoyed with these wonderful dishes.

なまこ酢
NAMAKO-SU

Vinegared Sea Cucumber

ナマコの旬は冬。熱燗にはぴったりの
大人のつまみ。こりこりと力強くはね
返す歯ごたえは、アワビにも勝る。

The best season for sea cucumber is winter.
Vinegared sea cucumber appeals to mature
palates and goes perfectly with hot sake. Sea
cucumber is even more pleasantly chewy than
abalone.

たこ酢
TAKO-SU

Vinegared Sea Cucumber

酢との相性は抜群。握りとは違うタコの
味わいを丸ごと楽しめる。しなやかな
弾力ある身は、噛むたびに甘みを増す。

Octopus and vinegar are made for each other.
Different from "nigiri", here you can enjoy the
taste and flavor of octopus by itself. As you
chew, the sweet flavor of the smooth but elastic
meat intensifies.

Vinegared Dishes

つまみ

Appetizers

はま吸い
HAMA-SUI

Clear Clam Soup

お吸い物の代表格。上品で香りが高く、
澄んだ汁にハマグリの旨味がぎゅっと
閉じ込められている。

Clear clam soup is the standard for clear soup.
This dish is elegantly flavorful. The delicious
essence of clam is perfectly infused into the
clear soup.

あさりの味噌汁
ASARI-NO-MISOSHIRU

Asari Clam Miso Soup

アサリの味を余すことなく味わえる。
独特の旨味が、味噌の風味と出合って、
まろやかに口に広がる。

You can fully enjoy the taste of the asari clam.
Its unique umami blends with miso and fills
your mouth with a mild, smooth flavor.

寿司に合う酒

まずはビールという人が多い。日本酒は冷酒も熱燗も
寿司に合う。焼酎も「麦・ソバ・芋」と多種あり、ス
トレートやロック、お湯やウーロン茶で割るなどがあ
る。最近はワインを注文する人も増えている。

There are many people who enjoy beer, but both chilled Japanese
sake and warmed sake go well with sushi. Another alcoholic drink,
shochu, can be distilled from a variety of ingredients including
"barley, buckwheat, and potato", and is served straight, on the
rocks, or mixed with something else such as hot water or oolong
tea. Recently, the number of people ordering wine is increasing.

ワイン
Wine

日本酒
Japanese Sake

ビール
Beer

焼酎
Shochu
（Distilled Spirit）

Chapter 3
Learning More
About Sushi

THE SUSHI
MENU BOOK

寿司の材料

寿司ダネ

赤身、白身、光り物、魚卵など。醤油、塩、煮きりなど、寿司ダネによって味わい方も異なる。

Sushi-dane
(Sushi Topping)
 Examples include red meat, white meat, silver-skinned fish, and fish roe. Depending on the sushi-dane, condiments such as soy sauce, salt, and nikiri are used differently.

酢飯

酢・塩・砂糖などを合わせて、炊き上がりのご飯に手早くまぜ、冷ましてから舟形に握る。

Vinegared Rice
A combination of vinegar, salt, and sugar is rapidly mixed into cooked rice. After it cools, the rice is squeezed into a boat-shaped rice ball.

海苔

巻寿司、軍艦巻に使う。上質なものは香り、つや、手触りが良い。

Nori
Nori is essential for maki-sushi (rolls) and battleship rolls. High-quality nori is flavorful, shiny, and has a smooth texture.

Sushi Ingredients

ワサビ

寿司ダネの味を引き立て、辛みがあり食欲を刺激
する。殺菌効果もある。香り高く、サメ皮でおろ
すと良い。

Wasabi

Wasabi brings out the flavor of the sushi topping,
and stimulates your appetite. It also inhibits
microbe growth. Wasabi is fragrant and spicy, and
is good when grated with a tool made of sharkskin.

甘酢ショウガ

寿司を食べた後、口の中の香りを消す。次の寿司
ダネを食べるときの口直しに良い。

Sweet Pickled Ginger

Sweet pickled ginger neutralizes the fragrance
that lingers on the tongue after eating sushi and
is perfect for cleansing your palate between each
sushi-dane.

茶葉

寿司店で出されるお茶には煎茶などを作るときに
切れ端になった「粉茶」が使われる。クセのない
味で、ほのかな香りが、寿司に合う。茶葉に湯を
注ぎ、お茶として飲む。

Chaba (Tea Leaf)

The tea served at sushi restaurants is chaba, or
"broken tea," which is a side product of teas such
as sencha (medium-grade tea). It has a plain flavor
and its subtle aroma goes well with sushi. Hot water
is poured over the chaba and it is drunk as tea.

Description of the Table Setting

① 醤油
Soy sauce

酢飯と寿司ダネを調和させ、素材の持ち味を引き出す調味料。生（き）のままも使うが、みりんなどを加えた煮きり醤油もある。

This is a condiment to balance the taste of the vinegared rice with the sushi topping, and to bring out the natural flavor of the ingredients. You can use it as is, or it is also simmered with ingredients such as mirin to make nikiri.

② 付け台
Tsuke-dai

寿司をのせる木製の器。店によっては、皿や葉蘭が使われることもある。

Tsuke-dai is the wooden serving platter on which your sushi is placed. Some sushi bars use a plate or an aspidistra plant leaf instead.

③ おしぼり
Oshibori
(Wet Towel)

寿司屋に入ると最初に供される。身を清めるように、手を拭く。また、寿司を手でつまんで食べる際に使う。

As soon as you enter the sushi bar, the first thing served to you is a wet towel. Use it to wipe your hands, as if cleansing your body. You also use it to clean your hands after eating sushi with your fingers.

④ お茶
Tea

寿司店では、茶葉ではなく粉茶を用いる。香りが少なく、寿司ダネの邪魔をしないためである。濃くて熱いお茶は、舌に残る魚の脂をスッキリさせる。

At sushi restaurants, instead of tea leaves, chaba, or "broken tea" is used because it has a subtle aroma that doesn't interfere with the flavor of the sushi toppings. Strong, hot tea washes away the fish oil that lingers on your palate.

⑤ 醤油皿
Sauce Dish

醤油を入れる皿。10センチ前後の大きさで、三寸皿、四寸皿とも言われる。お椀は手に持って食べるが、醤油皿は持たない。

This is a dish for soy sauce. The size is about 10 centimeters, so that it is also called 3-sun dish or 4-sun dish. Although it is acceptable to hold a bowl in your hand when you eat, you are not supposed to hold a sauce dish.

⑥ 箸
Chopsticks

日本の食文化を代表する箸。食事をすることを「箸をつける」という言い方もあるほど。もちろん箸を使わずに手を使って食べてもかまわない。

Chopsticks are a symbol of Japanese food culture. There is even an expression, "touching with chopsticks", which means to have a meal. Needless to say, you can eat sushi without chopsticks.

⑦ 汁物
Shiru-mono
(Soup)

お吸い物、みそ汁など、お椀に入った飲み物。店によって、日によって、汁の中に入れる具材は異なるので面白い。

Shiru-mono is soup in a bowl, including clear soup and miso soup. Interestingly, the ingredients in the soup differ depending on the sushi bar or the day.

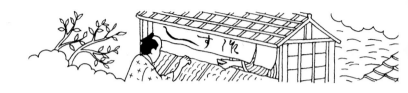

From Pre-Edomae Period to the Birth of Edomae-zushi

　寿司はもともと、保存のために考案された魚の漬け物「熟れ鮨（なれずし）」が原型。米や麦などの穀物を炊き、その中に魚を入れると、乳酸発酵の力で、穀物のでんぷんが分解されて酒になり、その後、酢となる。「魚肉・酸味・穀物」は、まさに寿司の原点である。

　熟れ鮨の発祥は、東南アジア。縄文時代の後期に稲作と共に、中国から日本へと伝わったと考えられている。年貢として納められた記録が残っていることから、当時は高貴な人たちだけの食べ物だったのだろう。

　室町時代以降は「早寿司」が誕生。熟れ鮨は発酵に数ヵ月以上かかるため、調味料として作られるようになった「酢」で、酸味を代用したのが始まり。早寿司は箱寿司となり、現在の押寿司、握り寿司へと発展する。

　江戸時代、妖術使いの手印を結ぶような素早さで酢飯を握り、江戸前で獲れる新鮮な魚介をのせた「握り寿司」が誕生。屋台に立ったままで口にほうり込む、手軽で便利で安い食べ物。せっかちで懐の寒い江戸っ子たちを熱狂させた。以後、屋台は店構えとなり、都会に溶け込んでいった。そして今、海を越えて世界の「SUSHI」として人気を高めている。

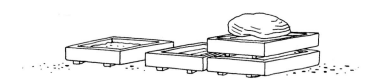

Sushi was originally invented as "nare-zushi", or pickled fish for preservation. Cooked grains such as rice and barley were packed into fish. Lactate fermentation decomposed the grains' starch into alcohol, which later became vinegar. The combination of "fish, acid, and grains" was definitely the origin of sushi.

Nare-zushi originated in Southeast Asia. It is believed that, at the end of the Jomon period, nare-zushi traveled from China to Japan along with rice cultivation. Considering that the remaining records show that nare-zushi was used as a tribute, nare-zushi seems to have been food for the nobles at that time.

After the Muromachi period, "haya-zushi" was born. Since it took more than several months of fermentation to make nare-zushi, "vinegar" was added as an ingredient and substituted for the acid. That was the beginning of haya-zushi. Haya-zushi became hako-zushi, and then developed into the current oshi-zushi and nigiri-zushi.

In the Edo period, "nigiri-zushi" was born. With eloquent hand motions vinegared rice is molded as quickly as a sorcerer casts a spell, and fresh fish from Tokyo Bay is placed on top of a rice ball. Nigiri-zushi, which was a convenient and cheap food you could eat while standing at a street stall, thrilled impatient locals who were low on funds. Since then, street stalls have transformed into permanent shops, which have blended into the urban city. And now, "SUSHI" is globally popular across the seas.

Ordering at a Sushi Restaurant

寿司店での会話

・「お好み」/「お任せ」/「お決まり」でお願いします。

Okonomi/omakase/okimari/de onegai shimasu.
I'll have "okonomi (your choice)"/ "omakase (chef's-
choice)"/ "okimari (set menu)".

※お好みで注文した場合、予算は 8,000 円くらいからが一般的です。
When you order your choice of sushi, it will usually cost you around 8,000 yen.

・私は貝 / エビは食べられません。

Watashi ha Ebi wa taberaremasen.
I cannot eat shellfish/ shrimp.

・ワサビはぬいてください。

Wasabi wo nuite kudasai.
No wasabi, please.

・何がおすすめですか？

Nani ga osusume desuka?
What do you recommend?

・ごちそうさまでした。

Gotisou sama desita.
That was a very good meal, thank you.

・お勘定お願いします。

Okanzyo wo onegai shimasu.
Check please.